Beginning Biographies

The Wright Brothers
The First to Fly

William Weir

PowerKiDS press™

NEW YORK

Published in 2013 by The Rosen Publishing Group, Inc.
29 East 21st Street, New York, NY 10010

Book Design: Katelyn Londino

Photo Credits: Cover Photo Researchers/Photo Researchers/Getty Images; p. 4 Apic/Contributor/Hulton Archive/Getty Images; pp. 5, 6, 9 Library of Congress; pp. 7, 8 Hulton Archive/Stringer/Hulton Archive/Getty Images; p. 10 commons.wikimedia.org/wiki/File:OrvilleInBikeShop.jpg/ Wikipedia.org; p. 11 NASA NASA/Photo Researchers/Getty Images; p. 12 Dorling Kindersley/Getty Images; pp. 13, 18 Hulton Archive/Stringer/Archive Photos/Getty Images; p. 14 commons.wikimedia.org/wiki/File:WrightBrothers1900Glider.jpg/Wikipedia.org; p. 15 National Archives/Handout/ Getty Images News; p. 16 Branger/Stringer/Hulton Archive/Getty Images; p. 17 commons.wikimedia.org/wiki/File:First_flight2.jpg/Wikipedia.org; p. 20 Science & Society Picture Library/Contributor/SSPL/Getty Images; p. 21 Mark Wilson/Getty Images News/Getty Images; p. 22 (Wilbur Wright) Fotosearch/Stringer/Archive Photos/Getty Images; p. 22 (boy with tools) Hemera/Thinkstock.com.

Library of Congress Cataloging-in-Publication Data

Weir, William, 1959-
The Wright brothers : the first to fly / William Weir.
    p. cm. — (Beginning biographies)
Includes index.
ISBN 978-1-4488-8863-4 (pbk.)
ISBN 978-1-4488-8864-1 (6-pack)
ISBN 978-1-4488-8597-8 (library binding)
1. Wright, Orville, 1871-1948—Juvenile literature. 2. Wright, Wilbur, 1867-1912—Juvenile literature. 3. Aeronautics— United States—Juvenile literature. 4. Inventors—United States—Biography—Juvenile literature. I. Title.
TL539.W394 2013
629.130092'273—dc23
[B]
                              2012013315

Manufactured in the United States of America

CPSIA Compliance Information: Batch #WS12RC: For further information contact Rosen Publishing, New York, New York at 1-800-237-9932.

Word Count: 488

Contents

A Great Team

The Wright brothers showed the world that people could fly! Wilbur and Orville Wright were the first people to fly in an airplane that they could **control**.

The Wright Family

Wilbur and Orville's parents were Milton and Susan Wright. They had two older brothers and one younger sister. Wilbur was born in Indiana on April 16, 1867.

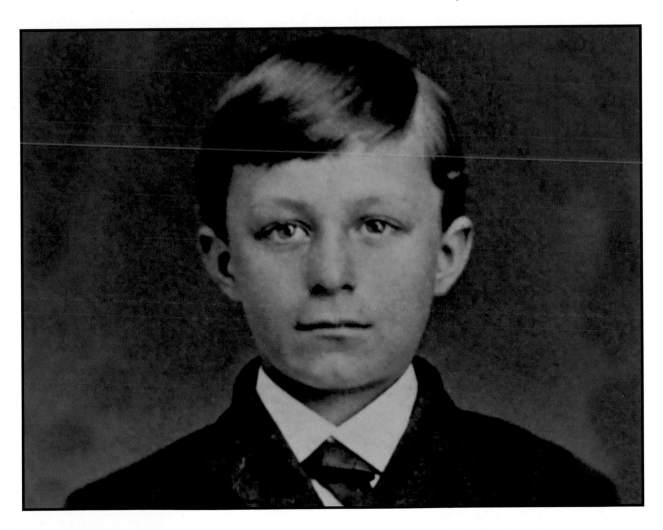

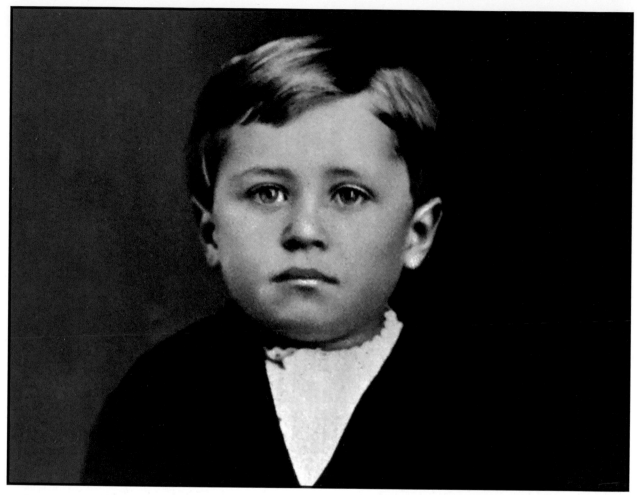

After Wilbur was born, Milton and Susan moved
with their children to the town of Dayton, Ohio.
Orville was born there on August 19, 1871.

Orville and Wilbur were very smart. They read lots of books while they were growing up. They liked to build things, too. The brothers were great builders.

Popular Printers

Orville and Wilbur built a machine to print newspapers and other papers. It's called a printing press. They used it to print two different newspapers.

The Wright brothers used this printing press in their
print shop. They opened the shop when Wilbur was 22
and Orville was 18. The shop was in Dayton.

Building Bicycles

Orville and Wilbur liked to work with other machines, too. They were good at fixing bicycles. Many people traveled on bicycles during this time.

The Wright brothers opened their own bicycle shop in 1892. At the shop, they fixed bicycles and worked on building new ones. In 1896, they built their own new bicycles.

Early Flying Machines

After they learned how to build bicycles,

the Wright brothers started to build flying machines.

They used kites to discover how to make things fly.

At that time, no one knew how to control
a flying machine. Wilbur and Orville discovered
that controlling the wings of the machine controlled
the way it moved.

The Wright brothers tested their first flying machine in 1900. It was called a **glider**. They traveled to Kitty Hawk, North Carolina, to test it.

The first glider flew in the air, but the Wright brothers still wanted to make a better flying machine. They made new gliders in 1901 and 1902.

Wilbur and Orville built an **engine** and two propellers for a new airplane. A propeller has **blades** that spin very quickly and move an airplane forward.

A Great Day for Flying

On December 17, 1903, Wilbur and Orville tested their new powered airplane at Kitty Hawk. Orville was the first one to fly it. The new airplane worked!

The Wright brothers became the first people to fly in a powered airplane that was heavier than air. They could control the machine, too. They flew their airplane four times that day.

First Flight Facts

December 17, 1903

flight number	Who flew?	How far did it fly?	How long did it fly?
flight 1	Orville	120 feet	12 seconds
flight 2	Wilbur	175 feet	12 seconds
flight 3	Orville	200 feet	15 seconds
flight 4	Wilbur	852 feet	59 seconds

Working Hard

After that day, the Wright brothers kept working.

In 1905, they built an airplane that could stay in the air for 39 minutes at a time and fly in circles!

Wilbur and Orville worked with airplanes for the rest of their lives. Wilbur died on May 30, 1912. Orville died on January 30, 1948. We still remember them today!

Changing the World

The Wright brothers were great **inventors**. We can fly on airplanes today because of the machines they built. Would you like to be an inventor someday?

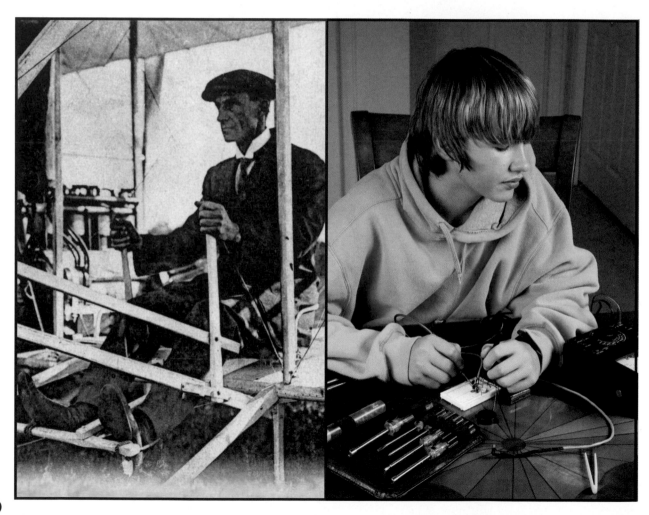

Glossary

blade (BLAYD) A flat, wide part.

control (kuhn-TROHL) To have power over something.

engine (EHN-juhn) A machine that makes things move.

glider (GLY-duhr) A flying machine that moves
without an engine.

inventor (ihn-VEHN-tuhr) A person who thinks up new
things to make or build.

Index

Due to the changing nature of Internet links, The Rosen Publishing Group, Inc., has developed an online list of websites related to the subject of this book. This site is updated regularly. Please use this link to access the list: **www.powerkidslinks.com/bbio/wbro**